D0853938

J 962 Tra
Tracy, Kathleen
We visit Egypt

LAP

$24.50
ocn780484069
07/31/2013

YOUR LAND AND MY LAND
AFRICA

We Visit

EGYPT

Kathleen

Tracy

Mitchell Lane
PUBLISHERS
P.O. Box 196
Hockessin, Delaware 19707

YOUR LAND
AND
MY LAND
AFRICA

Egypt
Ethiopia
Ghana
Kenya
Libya
Madagascar
Morocco
Nigeria
Rwanda
South Africa

LIBYA

EGYPT

Aswān

YOUR LAND
AND
MY LAND
AFRICA

We Visit

EGYPT

SUDAN

Gulf of Aden

Addis
Ababa ★

tasco

Mitchell Lane
PUBLISHERS

Copyright © 2013 by Mitchell Lane Publishers, Inc. All rights reserved. No part of this book may be reproduced without written permission from the publisher. Printed and bound in the United States of America.

Printing   1   2   3   4   5   6   7   8   9

Library of Congress Cataloging-in-Publication Data
Tracy, Kathleen.
 We visit Egypt / by Kathleen Tracy.
     p. cm. — (Your land and my land. Africa)
 Includes bibliographical references and index.
 ISBN 978-1-61228-301-2 (library bound)
 1. Egypt—Juvenile literature. I. Title. II. Series: Your land and my land (Mitchell Lane Publishers). Africa.
 DT49.T73 2013
 962—dc23
                                                        2012041879

eBook ISBN: 9781612283753

PUBLISHER'S NOTE: This story is based on the author's extensive research, which she believes to be accurate. Documentation of this research is on page 61.

   The internet sites referenced herein were active as of the publication date. Due to the fleeting nature of some websites, we cannot guarantee they will all be active when you are reading this book.

                                                                PLB

Contents

Introduction

The Dark Continent... the cradle of mankind... sometimes it seems as if Africa is a place lost in time. It certainly is a land of extremes. It produces more world-class diamonds than anywhere else on earth, and yet more than 2,500 children die there every day from a lack of clean water. Several African nations have established spectacular wild animal refuges, all of which are constantly endangered by ruthless poachers and inefficient policing. Africa boasts beautiful coastlines and beaches that belie the epidemic of poverty that ravages the sub-Saharan region. It has the newest country in the world, South Sudan, and one of the oldest with Egypt.

The second-largest continent on earth behind Asia, Africa is home to many modern cities such as Cairo, Nairobi, and Cape Town, but there are also millions of people who reside in small villages, living tribal lives nearly identical to the ones their ancestors lived centuries ago. According to the World Bank, less than 10 percent of the sub-Saharan population has access to electricity, and many are without indoor plumbing and running water.[1]

The continent's geography has created two distinct regions: North Africa and sub-Saharan Africa, which are divided by the Sahara

FYI FACT:

Before Africa was colonized, historians estimate that there were up to 10,000 independent states and groups, ranging in size from small clans of hunter-gatherers to large kingdoms such as Abyssinia (modern Ethiopia).[2]

Cairo, Egypt

Desert. Each area has a distinct culture, ethnicity, and landscape. Experts estimate that there are more than 2,000 languages spoken on the continent, but in North Africa, Arabic is the predominant language and Islam the main religion. The countries below the Sahara are less homogenous, so there are numerous languages spoken there. The different cultures have resulted in many tribal, or ethnic, disputes and tensions over many hundreds of years that persist to this day.

EGYPT

AFRICA

As a result, many sub-Saharan countries are mired in poverty and third world conditions, plagued by a lack of adequate food, high rates of AIDS, fewer opportunities for education, and political instability. And while many of those problems are also present above the Sahara, the countries of North Africa tend to have more developed infrastructures, stronger economies, and more Western influences. In this book we'll explore Egypt, one of Africa's most advanced nations and one of its oldest civilizations.

The Sahara is one of the hottest, driest places on earth. It receives an average of less than 3 inches (8 centimeters) of rain a year. It is also the world's biggest sand desert; it covers almost one-third of the African continent and is approximately the size of the continental United States.

Imagine living in a country covered almost entirely by an ocean of desert, much of it filled with sand dunes carved into artistic swirls and patterns by the desert winds, with some dune towers 400 feet (122 meters) tall. While such a landscape can be spectacularly beautiful, it is also essentially uninhabitable. Most of Egypt is made up of the Sahara, the world's largest hot desert, which is why over 95 percent of all Egyptians live along the Nile River. About half of those live in major cities like Cairo, Alexandria, and Luxor.

Egypt is located in the northeast corner of Africa and is approximately three times the size of New Mexico. Most of Egypt is located in Africa, but the Sinai Peninsula is technically considered part of Asia, and forms the only land bridge between the two continents. The northern border of Egypt lies along the Mediterranean Sea; to the west is Libya; to the south is Sudan; and along most of the eastern border lies the Red Sea, with the Gaza Strip and Israel to the east of the Sinai Peninsula.

In the most populated areas, the landscape of Egypt is generally flat and mostly at sea level. The highest elevations are found in the southwestern part of the country and along the southern Sinai Peninsula. Like its Middle Eastern neighbors, Egypt has a very dry, warm climate. But from June to October, the Nile floods, providing the population with much-needed water. If not for the Nile, the land making up Egypt would not be habitable, meaning the area now known as Egypt would have never been settled.

Did you know that Egypt is one of the oldest vacation destinations? The ancient Greeks used to travel to Egypt to marvel at the pyramids, the Sphinx, and the Lighthouse of Alexandria. Today, tourism is one of the country's most important industries and accounts for about 10 percent of Egypt's economy.

The global appeal of Egypt stems from its history. The Egyptian civilization is one of the oldest on earth, dating back more than 5,000 years. Ancient Egyptians were as dependent on the Nile as their modern counterparts are today. The river's annual floods provide the water and soil necessary for agriculture. The Nile flows in a northerly direction, from its beginnings in central Africa, and forms a delta 150 miles (240 kilometers) wide where it branches off and drains into the Mediterranean.

The Nile is more than 4,000 miles (6,000 kilometers) long and contains a series of rapids (known as cataracts) in its Great Bend. This portion of the Nile, where the river descends through narrow gorges, is an often impassable obstacle for boat traffic.

The United States has funded many agricultural programs to help Egyptian farmers increase production. Important crops include rice, cotton, and wheat.

Approximately one-third of Egyptian workers have jobs in farming. The warm climate enables farmers to plant several crops a year along the Nile.

Egypt is the third-most populous country in Africa, behind Nigeria and Ethiopia, and many of its citizens live in Cairo or Alexandria. Away from the cities, the land is largely deserted except for some small desert communities that are located around oases. The Egyptian government has developed irrigation to make some rural desert areas habitable, but in general, the cities are growing larger and the rural populations shrinking as people migrate to urban areas in search of work and a better standard of living.

Unlike Saudi Arabia, which has a highly diverse population due to high immigration numbers, Egypt is ethnically homogenous with a small immigrant population. But it is also a young country, with a

Voters line up in 2012, when millions of Egyptians voted in the first post-revolution elections.

median age of just twenty-four years old. The large number of young people in the country played a significant role in the 2011 political upheavals that forced long-time leader Hosni Mubarak to resign. In what is known as the Egyptian revolution, citizens demanded a democratic government process with less military involvement.

Although there have been occasional tensions in the past, the United States maintains a mutually beneficial trade relationship with Egypt. Approximately 12 percent of goods imported by Egypt come from the United States, and 8 percent of their exports go to America. In addition, Egypt's location and standing in the Middle East make it a strategically important political partner for the United States in maintaining stability in a notoriously volatile region.

FYI FACT:

The Sahara Desert is expanding to the south at a rate of 3 miles (5 kilometers) a year in a process called desertification, where soil turns into desert from a loss of moisture and vegetation.[1]

EGYPT FACTS AT A GLANCE

Steppe Eagle

Official Country Name: Arab Republic of Egypt
Official Language: Arabic
Population: 83,688,164 (July 2012 estimate)
Land Area: Approximately 386,662 square miles (1,001,450 square kilometers), slightly larger than three times the size of New Mexico
Capital: Cairo
Largest Cities: Cairo: 10.902 million; Alexandria: 4.387 million (2009 estimates)
Government: Republic
Ethnic Makeup: Egyptian 99.6%, other 0.4%
Religions: Muslim 90%, Coptic 9%, other Christian 1%
Main Exports: Petroleum, cotton, processed food, cotton, and metal products
Main Imports: Wheat, maize, wood products, cars and car spare parts
Crops and Agricultural Products: Cotton, rice, corn, wheat, beans, fruits, vegetables, cattle, water buffalo, sheep, goats
Climate: Hot, dry summers; moderate winters
Average Temperatures:
    Alexandria: January: 64°F (18°C) high, 52°F (11°C) low; August: 88°F (31°C) high, 73°F (23°C) low
    Cairo: January: 64°F (18°C) high, 46°F (8°C) low; July: 97°F (36°C), 70°F (21°C) low
Average Annual Rainfall:
    Alexandria: 7 inches (178 millimeters)
    Cairo: 1 inch (29 millimeters)
Lowest Point: Qattara Depression 436 feet (133 meters) below sea level
Highest Point: Mount Catherine 8,625 feet (2,629 meters) above sea level
Longest River: The Nile, which divides Egypt in two
National Flag: The current Egyptian flag, with red, white, and black horizontal stripes, was adopted on October 4, 1984. The red signifies bravery and the blood shed in past struggles; the white represents Egypt's bright future; and the black stands for determination over oppression. Inside the white stripe is the eagle of Saladin. A Muslim Sultan, Saladin ruled Egypt in the 12th century and is famous for uniting Egypt and Syria. He opposed the forces of the Crusaders, capturing many of their cities, including Jerusalem.
National Anthem: "Bilady, Bilady, Bilady" ("My Homeland, My Homeland, My Homeland")
National Sport: Soccer
National Flower: the Egyptian Lotus; also called the water-lily
National Bird: Steppe eagle

Source: CIA: *The World Factbook,* "Egypt"

Located about 65 miles (105 kilometers) north of Aswan, Edfu is home to the Temple of Horus, the falcon god. The temple, built during the Ptolemaic era, has been better preserved than any other temple in Egypt, according to experts.

Land of the Pharaohs

There is archaeological evidence that early hunter-gatherers lived in Egypt as far back as 12,000 BCE in the later Pleistocene epoch. The first permanent settlements occurred around 7000 BCE, although at the time, Egypt wasn't the desert it is today.

Back then, the Sahara was a very different place. According to geoarchaeologist Stefan Kröpelin from the University of Cologne in Germany, every 100,000 years the Sahara experiences 5,000 years of wetter, more humid weather. From about 8500 BCE to 3550 BCE, the Sahara was a green savanna that supported many kinds of life. "It was a good place to live," he says.[1]

But around 3500 BCE, the annual rainfall started decreasing. Kröpelin observes, "It's no coincidence that this major climate shift coincides with the rise of the early Egyptian empires. Only when the Sahara became a desert again did the emergence of the early Egyptian civilization occur."[2]

As the rain dwindled and the desert expanded, people established settlements all along the banks of the Nile, which is more than 4,000 miles (6,000 kilometers) long. Egypt at the time was divided into two kingdoms called Upper and Lower Egypt. But those designations were in terms of the river's flow, not geographical north and south. So Upper Egypt began at the Nile's rapids, or cataracts, and ended at the ancient

The Narmer Palette

city of Memphis; Lower Egypt consisted of the land from Memphis to the Mediterranean Sea.

Nobody knows definitively who united these two regions, making Memphis the capital of the new kingdom. Some ancient texts, such as the writings of the Greek historian Herodotus, refer to a king named Menes. But there has been no archaeological record found that mentions such a person. Many historians credit a leader named Narmer, who may have been the Greeks' Menes, with unifying Egypt around 3100 BCE. Their evidence is a piece of siltstone rock, called the Narmer Palette. On one side of the rock, a king identified as Narmer wears the red crown of Lower Egypt, and on the other side he's shown wearing the white crown of Upper Egypt.

The unification of Egypt is generally considered the beginning of the pharaoh lineage. For the next 3,000 years, Egypt would be ruled by pharaohs. Historians divide ancient Egyptian history into thirty dynasties. Each dynasty consists of a series of rulers belonging to the same family, much like the British monarchy where the current queen is from the house — or family — of Windsor, while King Henry VIII was a Tudor. When historians talk about Predynastic Egypt, they are referring to the time prior to the unification of the Upper and Lower regions.

The Egyptian dynasties are grouped into historical periods:

Early Dynastic Period: ca. 3100 - 2686 BCE (1st and 2nd Dynasties)
Old Kingdom: ca. 2686 - 2181 BCE (3rd to 6th Dynasties)
First Intermediate Period: ca. 2181 - 2040 BCE (7th to 10th Dynasties)
Middle Kingdom: ca. 2040 - 1797 BCE (11th and 12th Dynasties)
Second Intermediate Period: ca. 1797 - 1567 BCE (13th to 17th Dynasties)
New Kingdom: ca. 1567 - 1070 BCE (18th to 20th Dynasties)
Third Intermediate Period: ca. 1070 - 525 BCE (21st to 26th Dynasties)
Late Dynastic Period: ca. 525 - 332 BCE (27th to 30th Dynasties)

The era of the Old Kingdom was one of great advances. The first known major stone building, a step pyramid, was constructed in Saqqara for a Third Dynasty pharaoh named Zoser. The pyramid was designed by an architect named Imhotep, who built the interior of the pyramid to resemble Zoser's palace. Then, during the Fourth Dynasty, the Pyramids of Giza were built for pharaohs Cheops, Chephren, and Mycerinus. There were also many other pyramids built by crews of peasants recruited from all across Egypt, which is why the Old Kingdom is often referred to as the Age of the Pyramids.

After the reign of Userkaf during the Fifth Dynasty, there was a civil war led by some of the more powerful regional governors who were no longer loyal to the Pharaoh. The pharaohs that followed struggled to keep the kingdom united. A devastating fifty-year drought occurred between 2200 and 2150 BCE, which prevented the Nile from flooding and caused widespread famine and unrest. This ultimately led to a severely weakened central government and the eventual collapse of the Old Kingdom.

During the First Intermediate Period, which lasted around 200 years, Egypt was ruled by two competing monarchs; one located at Heracleopolis in the north, and another located in the south at Thebes, which is modern-day Luxor. The dueling pharaohs of this time only held power in their respective areas, meaning there was no centralized government. As such, no official records have been found from this era, but some writings have been found that indicate this was a period of lawlessness. Historians also believe it was during this time that most of the pyramids and tombs were robbed.

The Tenth Dynasty ruled Lower Egypt from 2130 to 2040 BCE, while the Eleventh Dynasty ruled Upper Egypt from 2134 to 1991 BCE. Sometime around 2040 BCE, the pharaoh in Thebes, Mentuhotep II, defeated the Heracleopolitan pharaoh, reunited Egypt under his throne, and became the first pharaoh of the Middle Kingdom. Mentuhotep II established Thebes as the capital.

The Middle Kingdom was a time of renaissance in art and literature. But the Thirteenth Dynasty brought instability to Egypt once

Pharaoh Nebhepetre Mentuhotep II ruled in the Eleventh dynasty for fifty-one years, and is credited with reuniting Upper and Lower Egypt. His statue, originally located outside of his temple at Deir el-Bahri, can now be seen at the Metropolitan Museum of Art in New York City.

again, marking the beginning of the Second Intermediate Period. During the Thirteenth Dynasty, Egypt had approximately sixty-five pharaohs over the course of 116 years. The revolving door of leaders enabled foreigners called the Hyksos to move into the Nile delta region and eventually take control of it.

The Fourteenth Dynasty included as many as seventy-six kings over the course of sixty years, but very little is known about any of these leaders. What is known is that the Fifteenth Dynasty was established by the Hyksos, who controlled the majority of the Nile delta and a lot of Upper Egypt. The majority of the Sixteenth Dynasty was also comprised of non-Egyptian rulers. But in the Seventeenth Dynasty, the Egyptian ruling house in Thebes declared its independence and initiated a war against the Hyksos, led by Tao II the Brave. Following his death, Tao's sons Kamose and Ahmose I continued to battle the Hyksos. Ahmose I is credited with finally driving the Hyksos out of the delta and establishing Theban rule over all of Egypt, marking the start of the Eighteenth Dynasty and the New Kingdom period.

Considered the second golden age of Egypt, the New Kingdom pharaohs expanded Egypt's empire, especially Tuthmosis III. Conquests and increased trade brought a lot of wealth to the country. It was during this period that the Valley of the Kings became *the* place to build tombs. Considered the most famous collection of such elaborate tombs, the Valley of the Kings lies on the Nile's west bank near modern day Luxor. Buried there were pharaohs, queens, high priests, and other elite members of the Eighteenth, Nineteenth, and Twentieth Dynasties.

The Valley is one of the most popular tourist destinations, where visitors can actually go into many of the sixty-four tombs, including the tomb of Tutankhamun, the boy king made famous by the discovery of his mummy.

Although he is the most famous of the pharaohs, there is actually very little known about him. It's believed he was the twelfth ruler of Egypt's Eighteenth Dynasty, ruling Egypt between 1334 and 1325 BCE. His birth name was Tutankhaten ("living image of Aten"), suggesting

King Tutankhamun in his stone sarcophagus in the Valley of the Kings

that his father was Akhenaten, who is known as the heretic pharaoh because he introduced the worship of one god, called Aten.

When Akhenaten died, Tutankhaten was made king — at nine years old. He changed his name to Tutankhamun in the second year of his reign after he reinstated the old Egyptian gods. But King Tut died when he was just eighteen or nineteen.

For all his modern notoriety, King Tut only ruled nine years. Ramses II (RAM-zeez), on the other hand, ruled for sixty-seven years, and during his reign Egypt was at the height of its empire. Ramses II is considered one of Egypt's greatest builders. In addition to having massive tombs built for himself and his wife, Ramses had most of the temples in the country upgraded or rebuilt. He is also famous for having sired as many as one hundred children.

The last great pharaoh of the New Kingdom period was Ramses III, who defended Egypt from a number of would-be invaders during his reign. The ongoing conflicts drained Egypt's treasury leading to the gradual, steady decline of the Empire. In the decades after Ramses III's death, the country was also hit with severe droughts, lower than usual flood levels, famine, public unrest, and political corruption. Ramses XI was the last of the New Kingdom leaders.

Kuwait
KUWAIT
Shiraz
Būshehr
Hafar
Land of the Pharaohs

2

During the Third Intermediate Period, pharaohs of Libyan descent came to power in the Twenty-second Dynasty, and rulers of Nubian descent founded the Twenty-fifth Dynasty. The country was attacked by the Assyrians in 671 BCE, and then by the Persians in 525 BCE, which marked the beginning of the Late Dynastic Period. The last dynasty ended when Egypt was conquered in 332 BCE by Alexander the Great and his Greek army.

With Alexander's death in 323 BCE, a Greek general named Ptolemy was appointed to oversee Egypt. Over time, Alexander's empire fell apart, and Ptolemy eventually made himself king of Egypt, founding the Ptolemaic dynasty, which ruled Egypt for around 300 years.

The most famous of the Ptolemaic rulers was Cleopatra, who was born in Alexandria in 69 BCE. When her father Ptolemy XII died in early 51 BCE, he left his kingdom to Cleopatra and her younger brother Ptolemy XIII, who was about eleven years old.

According to Egyptian law, Cleopatra could not rule the country on her own; she was required to have a consort, or partner. So she married her younger brother to comply with the law, and then proceeded to push him into the background. She took his name completely off official documents, even though male co-rulers were supposed to be named first. She had her name and portrait put on Egyptian coins but had none produced with her brother's name or likeness.

Her claim to fame was her personal life. She had relationships with Roman general Julius Caesar, and after Caesar was murdered, with Roman politician Marc Antony, who divorced his wife to go

Michelangelo's drawing of Cleopatra

WHERE IN THE WORLD IS EGYPT?

Where in the World

live with Cleopatra in Egypt. This did not sit well with people back in Rome. At the time Antony controlled the eastern half of Roman territory, and Octavian controlled the western half. Eventually, Octavian led troops against Cleopatra and Antony. When it became clear he would be defeated, and believing that Cleopatra was dead, Antony literally fell on his sword to commit suicide.

Octavian announced plans to make Cleopatra a slave and display her in public in chains. So Cleopatra had an Egyptian cobra, or asp, placed in her chambers and committed suicide by allowing the snake to bite her. Her death in 30 BCE marked the end of the dynasties in Egypt and the beginning of Roman rule in Egypt.

In 640 CE, Egypt was invaded by an Arab army that drove out the Romans in 642, making Egypt part of an Islamic empire that was later run by the Abbasid family. After being conquered by the Arabs, most Egyptians eventually converted from Christianity to Islam; those that didn't convert are called Copts. In the late 900s, a new family, the Fatimids, seized the Nile Valley. The Fatimids established a new palace city and named it al-Qaahira, or Cairo.

Around 1516, Egypt became part of the Islamic Ottoman Empire and remained under Turkish rule until the British occupied Egypt in 1882, seeking control of the Suez Canal. Egypt was granted independence from Britain in 1922, although English troops stayed to guard the canal until 1956. It wasn't until the last of the British soldiers had left that the people of Egypt felt truly independent.

Like many Islamic states, Egypt had tense relations with Israel in the latter half of the 20th century. This led to armed conflict in the Six-Day War, in which Israel defeated Egyptian, Syrian, Jordanian, and Iraqi forces in literally less than a week. In 1978, the two countries signed the groundbreaking Camp David Accords, which brought peace between the two countries. Although Egypt may have succeeded in finding compromise with its neighbor, it still faced ongoing internal conflicts that would shape the country's future.

FYI FACT:

Pharaohs never allowed their hair to be seen, and wore a crown or a headdress called a nemes.

Known as the father of modern Egypt, Mohammed Ali came to the country as an Albanian commander in the Ottoman army. He eventually declared himself the official leader of Egypt, and helped the country transition into the modern world.

Chapter 3

The Arab Spring

Egypt has had many different governments over the course of its long history. It has enjoyed extended periods of stability and growth, but it has also suffered through many years of political instability. The unrest that frequently punctuated Egyptian life in ancient and historical times also plagues modern Egypt as it struggles to establish an independent, democratic republic.

For over 300 years the Turks of the Ottoman Empire controlled Egypt, and it was an Ottoman commander who is often called the father of modern Egypt. Mohammed Ali was an officer in the regiment that was sent to take control of Egypt following France's occupation of Egypt from 1799-1802.

After Napoleon and the French army retreated, there was widespread political unrest in Egypt, with regional factions at odds with each other. None of the governors sent from Istanbul were able to restore order. Eventually, city leaders approached Ali and asked for help, offering him their support and loyalty. Once he took control of the local administration, Ali secured the support of native Egyptian religious leaders, guild officials, and the upper class. In 1805 he declared himself pasha, a Turkish title meaning leader, and was recognized by the Turkish sultan as the official governor of Egypt.

While Ali is credited with unifying Egypt and turning it into a modern country, his actions were not altruistic. He wanted to establish a power base to create his own empire. But in so doing, he did many things that also helped Egypt. He ruthlessly eliminated opposition, then stabilized the country by centralizing the government in Cairo and training a new army, which helped re-establish law and order. Ali enacted agricultural policies, increasing the amount of land available for cultivation by a million acres, and upgrading the canal system.

But after his death in 1849, there was a political power void that eventually led to Egypt's occupation by Britain in 1882. Between 1922, when Egypt became technically independent from the British Empire, and 1956, when the last of the British soldiers left, there were three main political groups vying for power: the Wafd, a political organization opposed to British influence; King Fuad, who had been awarded the throne by the British when they granted Egypt independence; and the British, who were determined to stay in Egypt to maintain control of the Suez Canal.

In July 1952, a group of army officers led by Lt. Col. Gamal Abdel Nasser overthrew King Fuad's son and successor, King Farouk. A year later Egypt was declared a republic organized by Nasser, who later became a respected leader in the Arab world. But his reputation was tarnished by Egypt's humiliating defeat at the hands of Israel in the 1967 Six-Day War.

Nasser died three years later in 1970, and was succeeded by Anwar Sadat, who instituted economic reforms by easing governmental con-

Nasser carrying his unit's flag in 1940.

trols and encouraging private investment and enterprise. Sadat also rooted out corrupt government officials and put them on trial. While his efforts strengthened the Egyptian government, improvements came at a cost. On October 6, 1981, Islamic extremists assassinated Sadat, and Vice President Hosni Mubarak took over as President.

Once he was in power, Mubarak's attention moved away from his stated goals of economic expansion and political reform. Instead, opposition to Mubarak was repressed and he declared a long-running state of emergency that gave him almost total dictatorial control.

The first competitive presidential elections were not held until 2005. Mubarak was re-elected amidst charges of voter fraud. A similar situation occurred again in 2010. Angered by what they perceived as a corrupt government, protesters gathered in Cairo's Tahrir Square. The crowd grew into a passionate mob that turned into a political revolution.

Mubarak was forced to resign and a transitional government was established that was led by the Supreme Council of the Armed Forces (SCAF). On March 19, 2011, Egyptians voted overwhelmingly to amend Egypt's constitution so there could be democratic parliamentary and presidential elections. The ballot also included term limits for the president and judicial oversight of voting.

In June 2012, Mohamed Morsi of the Muslim Brotherhood was declared the winner of Egypt's first competitive presidential election. However, in October 2012, the *New York Times* reported Egyptians were protesting against the Muslim Brotherhood, demanding that the current Constitution be dissolved and that Islamists stop "foisting their ideas on society," a sign that the road to democracy remains a work in progress for one of the world's most storied cultures.

FYI FACT:

Egyptian tomb workers went on the first known labor strike during the reign of Ramses III. They stopped working to protest a lack of adequate food, which was their payment for building the pharaoh's tomb.

Boating on the Nile River is a popular activity for both tourists and residents. Cruises offer passengers the chance to see Egypt while sailing along the longest river in the world.

Flora and Fauna

Egypt may not have the most diversity when it comes to topography, but its landforms have played an integral role in the country's history and development. The two main geographic features of Egypt are its deserts and the Nile.

Located in the northeast corner of Africa, Egypt is literally divided in two by the Nile River. To the west of the Nile is the Libyan or Western Desert, which is actually part of the Sahara. This desert area has several known oases including Siwa, Dakhla, Bahariya, Farafra, and Kharga. At least one oasis, called the Fayoum, has been around since the time of the pharaohs.

To the east of the Nile is the Eastern Desert. Also called the Arabian Desert, it extends to the Red Sea Hills, a series of mountains whose highest peak is the 7,175-foot (2,187-meter) tall Mount Shaiyb al-Banat. Most of the people who live in this eastern region reside in small communities between the Red Sea and the Red Sea Hills and make their living fishing, mining, or working in the oil industry. The Eastern Desert is rich in natural resources, with oil fields and mineral and metal deposits including phosphate, uranium, and gold.

The Sinai Peninsula is a plateau featuring deep valleys and several mountains in the southern area including Egypt's highest point, Mount Catherine at 8,668 feet (2,642 meters) and Mount Sinai, where, according to the bible, Moses received the ten commandments from God. The northern end of the peninsula is mostly a sand desert.

There are many varieties of egrets in different parts of the world, including the Great Egret, which is common in Egypt. At one time, many species of egrets were endangered, as their feathers were valuable to hat makers.

The delta is a vast, lush area that is home to many plants and animals. Every winter, hundreds of thousands of birds migrate to the delta, including the world's largest number of little gulls and whiskered terns. The delta is home to approximately 300 species of birds including gray herons, egrets, and ibises.

But there are far fewer wild four-legged animals in Egypt. The delta has frogs, turtles, mongooses, wild boars, and the Nile monitor lizard. Nile crocodiles, wild boars, and hippopotamuses are no longer found in the delta, although crocodiles have habitats around Lake Nasser, which is south of the Aswan Dam. Egypt also has populations of desert gazelles, ibexes, hyenas, jackals, and lynxes. There are more than thirty types of snakes in Egypt, including several poisonous species such as the horned viper, saw-scaled viper, and asp (Egyptian cobra), the snake made famous by Cleopatra's suicide.

The most common domesticated animals are camels, sheep, and goats. Cows are also raised in Egypt, but they're less common, mostly

The camel actually originated in North America and eventually migrated to Asia and the Middle East, crossing the Bering Strait. When the camel first came to Africa, it was only around 3 feet (1 meter) tall.

FYI FACT:

Ancient Egyptian hunters took their cats along and trained them to catch birds and fish, much like dogs are used today by modern hunters.

because the climate is so dry and they require grassland for grazing. Sheep and goats fare better in the desert climate.

There are very few forests in Egypt, but there are date palm groves. Citrus groves and eucalyptus and cypress trees have also been introduced. The most common flowering plants are lotuses, irises, lilies, jasmine, and roses. Papyrus used to be plentiful, but is becoming increasingly rare because other species of plants have taken over its native habitat, the delta.

Despite the hot climate, the inland desert areas can experience wild temperature fluctuations, reaching well over 100°F (38°C) during the day, but dropping to the mid-40s (7°C) at night. Similarly, the area closest to the Mediterranean gets around 8 inches (20 centimeters) of rain a year, but the southern regions average less than an inch (3 centimeters) of rain annually. The northern area of the Eastern Desert is so dry that hardly any plant life can survive. There is more humidity in the southern portion of the desert, so a handful of trees and shrubs grow there.

Acacia tree in the Eastern Desert

Completed in 1970, the Aswan Dam was built to control the annual flooding of the Nile River. The dam created Lake Nasser, which has spurred a growing fishing industry in Egypt.

The Nile supports over one hundred species of fish and the Red Sea has plentiful coral and tropical marine fish. The Aswan Dam was constructed to provide irrigation water and electricity, and also created a healthy fish industry. But it has also had unintended environmental consequences. For thousands of years, sediment was spread by the yearly flooding of the Nile – but that sediment is now trapped behind the dam. As a result, the fertility of the land downstream from the dam has diminished.

For thousands of years, the nomadic Bedouins have shepherded their herds across the Sahara. While the number of Bedouin herders is growing smaller, many continue to carry on the tradition, relying on oases for refuge from the desert heat and sun.

Walk Like
an Egyptian

Compared to most Western countries like the United States, Britain, or France, Egypt is not a particularly diverse country. More than 99 percent of the population is ethnically Egyptian. The remaining 1 percent is mostly made up of Armenians, Greeks, Italians, French, and Nubians. There is also a small population of nomadic Bedouins, an Arabic people who still shepherd their herds across the harsh desert landscape as their ancestors did thousands of years ago. The Bedouins are found in both the Eastern and Western Deserts, as well as the Sinai Peninsula.

In countries like Saudi Arabia, foreign nationals make up nearly one-quarter of the population, drawn by the job opportunities presented by the Saudis' massive oil production. Egypt, however, has relatively few foreign nationals taking up residence there. While the country remains a popular tourist destination for people from all over the world, there are not many business opportunities to attract foreign nationals. Plus, in the aftermath of Mubarak's ouster, the government stopped renewing temporary visas for the few foreign nationals who were there already.

The majority of Egyptians are Muslim, but between 8 and 15 percent are Copts, a Christian denomination unique to Egypt. In 1971, the government made Islam the official state religion. While the Egyptian Constitution grants religious freedom, it's only protected as long as it does not conflict with Islamic law. There is a long history

Until it was invaded by Arab Muslims in 640 CE, Egypt was a Christian country. In 1971, Egypt officially declared Islam the state religion. Today, approximately 90 percent of Egyptians are Muslim and just 10 percent are Christian.

of religious discrimination in Egypt, as well as tensions and confrontations between Islamic fundamentalists and Copts.

The Muslim influence is also seen in Egypt's choice of official language, Arabic. It is estimated that there are more than 200 million native speakers of Arabic worldwide. And because it is the language of the Quran, even more Muslims are versed in it, even if it is not their native tongue.

But spoken Arabic varies from country to country, and is often subdivided into the following categories: Classical, Modern Standard, Eastern Colloquial, and Western Colloquial. The Quran uses classical Arabic, which was the dialect used in Mecca. Egypt's dialects are part of the Eastern Colloquial Arabic family.

According to the Tour Egypt website, "The main dialects that have been identified in Egypt and Eastern Libya include: Delta Arabic, Lower Egypt Arabic, Middle Egypt Arabic, Upper Egypt Arabic, Cairene Arabic, and others. Within these categories there are further regional sub-varieties. The differences among all the dialects are minor and, as a rule, do not impair understanding."[1]

However, dialects from different countries can be so different as to hinder communication. So, Modern Standard Arabic (MSA) was established as the general dialect used for conversation. Based on Classical Arabic, MSA is also used in books, magazines, and newspapers, as well as on television and radio. The dialect of Cairo, known as Cairene Arabic, is also widely understood among people living in major urban areas of the Arabic-speaking world.

Egypt's ties to the Arab world through religion and language make it seem as though Egyptians might identify more with the Middle East than Africa. But modern Egyptians do not consider themselves Arabic *or* African.

A former exchange student at the American University in Cairo, Carla Daughtry explains: "In 1988, I was one of twenty college year abroad students at the American University in Cairo... I learned that most Egyptians do not consider themselves African and, even less so, Black African. I learned that some Egyptians do not even consider themselves Arab; they have a home-grown notion of identity: Egyptians are Egyptians."[2]

But for many years, not all Egyptians were treated equally when it came to education, which through most of the 20th century was a luxury reserved only for the elite class. While the government has established many programs designed to give more people the opportunity to attend school, progress has been slow. According to the Central Intelligence Agency, as of 2005, just 71 percent of the population could read and write; and only 59 percent of females age fifteen and older were literate.

It is ironic the country has such a high illiteracy rate, because archaeological findings suggest that Egyptian hieroglyphics is the oldest form of writing, probably predating even the Sumerians' cuneiform writing. The oldest known hieroglyphs date back to around 3300 BCE, and were found on clay tablets in a tomb.

Hieroglyphics is a system of writing that uses pictures or symbols to represent specific objects like the sun, abstract ideas like heat, or sounds. Symbols used to represent objects or ideas are called pictograms. And a symbol used to describe a sound is called a phonogram. Egyptians created words by combining both types of symbols.

The word hieroglyph comes from the Greeks, meaning "sacred carving," and was originally used to describe the markings they found adorning Egyptian monuments. Now hieroglyphs refer specifically to the Egyptians' writing system. But initially only a small percentage of Egyptians — clergy, government officials, and royalty — used hieroglyphs because they were hard to learn and took a long time to create.

Ancient Egyptians used between 700 and 800 basic symbols, called glyphs, written right to left, left to right, or from top to bottom. There was no spacing or punctuation used to separate words or ideas. There also were no vowels, so pronunciation just using hieroglyphics isn't possible. However, other civilizations like the Sumerians wrote about the Egyptians, so historians have been able to figure out the names of many pharaohs from their writings. But the biggest breakthrough in translating hieroglyphics was the discovery of the Rosetta Stone by Napoleon's army during their invasion of Egypt.

The Rosetta Stone contained the same inscription written in ancient hieroglyphics and demotic script, along with the Greek translation. That gave linguists the information they needed to "crack" the hieroglyph code. Prior to that, because hieroglyphs had fallen out of use, nobody knew how to decipher them.

In general, Egyptologists now classify Ancient Egyptian writing into three categories based on appearance. Hieroglyphic is the pictoral style found on monuments and religious texts. Hieratic is a cursive style found in books and documents and is believed to have been also

FYI FACT:

Nubia was an ancient African kingdom located in what is present-day northern Sudan and southern Egypt. Some of the old Nubian land was flooded after the construction of the Aswan Dam and is now under Lake Nasser.

Hieroglyphic writing

used by priests. Basically, hieratic is a simpler form of the hieroglyphic type. Demotic is cursive script that replaced hieratic as the everyday style after 600 BCE.

From hieroglyphs and other sources, we know that in ancient Egypt, women of the right social class were considered equal to their male peers. They were granted the same legal and financial rights, and as evidenced by Cleopatra, could even rule the country. In other words, equality was based primarily on social class and not gender.

Even today, Egyptian women have much more freedom and opportunity than women in fundamentalist Muslim countries such as Saudi Arabia. Women in Egypt can drive cars and wear regular clothes instead of burqas, which would cover the women from head to toe. They can also go to college, earn professional degrees, and work as lawyers and doctors. But their overall rights are still not equal to those of men. Women in Egypt often are the victims of domestic violence that goes unprosecuted, experience job discrimination, and have very little political presence. It's not surprising, then, that women had a major presence in the protests that led to the new government; one they hope will eventually grant all citizens true equality.

When the Cairo Opera Ballet Company was established in 1966, its members were initially coached by Soviet dancers and choreographers. Its inaugural production was *The Fountain of Bakhchisarai.*

Culture

Egypt is a unique blend of the ancient and the modern. Its modern culture isn't so much informed by the past as it is an extension of it. For example, many of the aspects of the art, music, and dance enjoyed by today's Egyptians originated in the time of the pharaohs 5,000 years ago. But despite deeply rooted ties with the ancient empire, much of Egypt is very contemporary, with fine restaurants, high-end stores, world-renowned museums, and national teams for sports like soccer and squash.

The Cairo Opera House is one of the capital's newest venues. Opened in 1988, the Opera House was built to promote modern music and dance and to preserve traditional music. The Opera House is part of the National Cultural Centre, which was founded to "give space to learning and inspiration, to the exchange of ideas, the respect of a common cultural heritage, and a shared passion for the arts. It encourages interest for music and art in the younger generation by offering ballet, voice or instrumental classes for talented children or youths."[1]

The Opera House presents ballet, opera, and symphony performances from both Egyptian companies and foreign troupes. In-house companies travel throughout the country so residents in other areas can enjoy the arts.

Egypt also has a thriving film industry, giving Cairo the title of "Hollywood of the Middle East." Approximately 3,000 movies have been filmed here, and the Cairo International Film Festival was ranked one of the top eleven festivals by the International Federation of Film Producers' Associations.

Egyptian writers, especially novelists and poets, are considered among the most innovative in Arab literature, and their style has influenced writers in countries around the world. In 1988, for example, Cairo-born novelist Naguib Mahfouz was the first Arabic-language writer to win the Nobel Prize in Literature. There are also well-known female Egyptian writers, including Nawal El Saadawi and Alifa Rifaat, both of whom write about women's issues.

While the original library at Alexandria may no longer exist, the city has a state-of-the-art new library, which opened in 2002. Shaped like a giant disc, it has what's billed as the largest reading space in the world, furnished with more than 2,000 reading chairs. The building is adorned in scripts and letters from nearly every language to symbolize the multicultural heritage and spirit of the library. When fully stocked, the library will house more than eight million books.

Library of Alexandria

FYI FACT:

Cairo has the only subway on the continent of Africa.

One of the most fascinating features of the library is CULTURAMA, an interactive attraction that displays Egypt's cultural heritage on nine huge computer screens arranged in a panoramic, semi-circular shape. Visitors are invited to explore a 5,000-year timeline by clicking on specific items or dates to reveal more in-depth information on the screen.

A blend of indigenous, Arabic, Western, Mediterranean, and African sounds, Egyptian music reflects the country's multifaceted historical influences. Traditional music is often played with a harp and native Egyptian instruments, including the flute-like *ney,* and the *oud,* a wooden stringed instrument related to the lute. Egyptian folk music, which is still played at weddings, festivals, and other traditional events, is extremely varied, with each region having its own distinct style. Contemporary music is most similar to pop and techno, and is mostly embraced by younger Egyptians.

Cairo has a vibrant nightlife, with a multitude of music and dance clubs that attract visitors and locals alike. Some of the most popular spots are those with belly dancers. Interestingly, it is still illegal to dance in public with an uncovered navel in Egypt, so belly dancers wear a body stocking if their costume exposes their midriff.

When visiting Egypt, it's important to be mindful of local customs and etiquette, whether you agree with them or not. Traveling to another country is a chance to see daily life from a different perspective. For example, all Muslims are required to pray five times a day: before dawn, at noon, afternoon, sunset, and evening. Don't be surprised to see people stop what they are doing to pray, facing Mecca.

While foreign men and women are not expected to wear Arab garments, it is respectful to dress modestly, especially for women, keeping legs and shoulders covered. Wearing shorts and a bikini top, the way people might in Miami or Los Angeles, would be inappropriate in Egypt.

Taking photographs of bridges and canals — including the Suez Canal — is illegal. Likewise, it is against the law to take photos of soldiers, military buildings, embassies, and equipment.

Take the time to learn some basic Arabic phrases, such as *salam* ("hello"), *shukran* ("thank you"), or *kaif halak?* ("how are you?"). The effort will be appreciated and well-received. If you are invited to an Egyptian's house, it's customary to bring a small thank-you gift. Avoid giving flowers because they are traditionally used only for funerals and weddings. But any kind of sweet or chocolate is good. And when giving the gift, remember to use your right hand (or both hands); to Arabs, the left hand is unclean.

When eating in a private residence, do not clean your plate. Always leave a little bit of food to show you've had enough to eat. Again, when eating, use only your right hand. Egyptian cuisine is flavorful, and traditional dishes use meat, rice, vegetables, and spices. One of the country's most popular dishes is koshary, made with pasta, rice, lentils, chickpeas, onions, and garlic. To find out what it tastes like, try out the recipe at the back of the book!

Depending on what time of year you visit Egypt, you may encounter one of several religious events. *Eid al-Adha,* the "Feast of Sacrifice," is an Islamic festival that commemorates Abraham's willingness to follow Allah's command to sacrifice his son. Eid al-Adha is observed

Dining out in Egypt is popular too.

at the end of the annual *Hajj,* which is the yearly pilgrimage to Mecca in Saudi Arabia. According to Islamic law, Muslims must make the trip at least once in their life, unless prevented by some financial hardship or physical incapacitation.

Eid al-Adha begins on the tenth day of Dhul-Hijja, the twelfth month of the Islamic lunar year. In most places, the Eid al-Adha celebration lasts several days. The exact dates of the Feast vary in different countries. That is because in some parts of the world, Islamic months begin at sunset on the day when the lunar crescent first appears after the new moon, and can be seen with the naked eye. Visibility depends on unpredictable factors such as weather conditions so Eid al-Adha has typically been celebrated on different days in various areas of the world. In Egypt, however, the new month begins based on calculations of the phases of the moon which don't rely on visibility. Also, because Islamic dates are based on a lunar calendar, each year the Feast of Sacrifice is observed about eleven days earlier than the year before.

The month of Ramadan is a time of personal reflection, spiritual renewal, and strict fasting – eating, drinking, and sexual intimacy are prohibited during the daylight hours of Ramadan, but feasting after nightfall and before dawn is allowed. At the end of Ramadan, Egyptian Muslims observe an exuberant three-day celebration called *Eid al-Fitr,* the "Festival of Fast-Breaking."

Before the start of Eid, each Muslim family gives a donation of food to the poor, such as rice, barley, and dates, to ensure that even needy Muslims can have a holiday meal and participate in the celebration. This charitable donation is known as *sadaqah al-fitr,* "charity of fast-breaking."

Eid al-Fitr falls on the first day of Shawwal, the month that follows Ramadan in the Islamic calendar. In other words, it celebrates the conclusion of Ramadan's intense introspection. Muslims gather during early morning in outdoor locations or mosques to perform the Eid prayer, which is followed by a sermon. After the prayer is finished, everyone leaves to visit family and friends. It is common to give gifts, especially to women and children.

Egypt's year-round moderate climate is perfect for growing cotton. The commercial cultivation of cotton began during the reign of Mohammed Ali. Egyptian cotton quickly gained popularity in Europe, and eventually, the rest of the world.

Economy and Commerce

For most of Egypt's history, cotton was grown primarily as a decorative plant. It wasn't until the early 19th century that Mohammed Ali directed the first large-scale planting of cotton for commercial use. It was discovered that the Egyptian soil gave the cotton exceptional fineness and strength. As word of this unique cotton spread, demand increased. In 1849, Egypt was exporting 87,000 bales of cotton yearly, with each bale weighing 500 pounds. By 1865, the United States was fighting the Civil War, and wasn't producing much cotton. To meet demand, Egypt exported 439,000 bales that year. Today, Egypt produces around 500,000 bales annually.

Sugar is the most commonly produced crop, however most is consumed locally, so its value as a commodity is limited. But maize, tomatoes, wheat, rice, potatoes, and dates are important exports. In recent years, Egypt has significantly increased its exports of oranges and tangerines, as well.

Even though tobacco is not grown in the country, Egyptian cigarettes are famous the world over. Tobacco is imported and blended in Egypt. The resulting cigarettes are exported around the world.

One of the most important Egyptian industries is tourism, which sharply declined after the protests that resulted in President Mubarak's resignation in 2011, and the ongoing protests in other Middle Eastern countries. Tourism rates only started to rise again in the summer of 2012, giving the country's economy a much-needed boost.

While living conditions vary within the country, many Egyptian children live in poverty.

Like many African nations, Egypt's population is young, with over 60 percent of the populace thirty years old and under, and a high number of young people are unemployed. Living conditions for the average Egyptian remain poor and more than 20 percent of the population lives below the poverty line. A report from the United Nations Children's Fund found that conditions for children have especially deteriorated.

"The income gap in Egypt has steadily increased since 2000, and almost seven million children were living below the income poverty line in 2008," the report states. "This is almost 1.3 million children more than about ten years earlier."[1]

In some areas, it is not uncommon for groups of children to approach tourists and ask for money. Visitors are discouraged from giving money because it could cause a mob to form.

One of Egypt's biggest problems is that its population continues to grow, which puts a strain on its most important natural resource, the Nile, and creates increasing competition for the jobs that are available. Even though Egypt has enjoyed economic growth in the 21st century, it has not been enough to keep up with its increasing population. In addition to the challenges of restoring order and establishing democracy in the country, Egypt's post-revolution leaders will also face the challenge of bringing economic stability to this growing nation.

FYI FACT:

Poor individuals and families who cannot afford to pay high rents go to live in al-Arafa, a cemetery, where they move into the tombs and mausoleums. As a result, the area is called City of the Dead.

As a female scholar who was not Christian, Hypatia attracted as many critics as she did followers. This didn't stop people from all over the world from traveling to hear her speak, however.

Chapter 8

Famous Egyptians, Past and Present

Egyptian history is full of well-known leaders such as Cleopatra, King Tut, and Mohammed Ali. But there are many accomplished Egyptians from other fields, as well.

Hypatia

Hypatia of Alexandria is considered the first female mathematician. Born around 370 CE, Hypatia was tutored by her mathematician father. When she was older, Hypatia attended school in Greece where she earned her reputation as a talented mathematician. She returned to Alexandria and was offered a position teaching mathematics and philosophy at the university where her father had worked. She was a prolific writer, producing many math textbooks, and people came from all over the world to hear her lectures.

Hypatia's philosophic and religious beliefs were in conflict with the Christian religion of the time. In March 415, a mob of Christians attacked Hypatia on her way to the university. They took her to a church where they dismembered her, then burned the pieces of her body. Her legacy inspired free thinkers and scientists for centuries.

Omar Sharif

Omar Sharif is a world-famous Egyptian actor. He was born Michel Demitri Shalhoub on April 10, 1932, in Alexandria. He attended Victoria College and Cairo University and earned degrees in math and physics. After graduating from college, Michel went to work at his

Sharif as Sherif Ali ibn
el Kharish in the David
Lean film, *Lawrence of
Arabia.*

father's lumber business, but his friends were people in the film business. He met a film director who in 1953 offered him a part in a movie, *Struggle in the Valley (Siraa fil Wadi).* The film was a critical hit, but more importantly, Sharif fell in love with his leading lady, Faten Hamama, and the couple married two years later in 1955. Later that year, their son Tarek was born. Raised Catholic, Michel converted to Islam in order to marry Hamama and at that time changed his name to Omar Sharif.

In 1962, Sharif became an international star for his role in *Lawrence of Arabia,* which earned him an Academy Award nomination. His dashing good looks made him a Hollywood heartthrob and he starred in many movies, including *Doctor Zhivago* and *Funny Girl.*

At the height of his movie stardom, Sharif also gained fame as a world-class professional card player in bridge. He would go on to write a newspaper column and author several books on the subject. In 1991, the Omar Sharif on Bridge computer game was released. He has since retired from gambling, saying he had lost quite a bit of money.

After several years away from acting, he made a comeback in 2003 playing the title role of an elderly Muslim shopkeeper in the French film, *Monsieur Ibrahim*. His performance earned Sharif the Best Actor Award at the Venice Film Festival and the César, France version of the Academy Awards.

Today, Sharif lives in Egypt.

Ayman al-Zawahiri

While his name may not be as recognizable as Osama bin Laden's, Ayman al-Zawahiri is one of the FBI's Most Wanted Terrorists. A member of al-Qaeda, there is a $25 million reward for information leading to his arrest.

After the death of Osama bin Laden in June 2011, Ayman al-Zawahiri took over as the head of al-Qaeda and became Number One on the FBI's Most Wanted list.

Ayman Mohammed Rabie al-Zawahiri was born on June 19, 1951, in Maadi, Egypt. His upper-class family consisted of many doctors and scholars, so al-Zawahiri grew up highly educated. He graduated from Cairo University's medical school in 1974, and received his master's degree in surgery in 1978.

Al-Zawahiri was politically active from his youth, joining his first extremist group when he was just fourteen. After getting his college degree, al-Zawahiri founded another radical group, the Egyptian Islamic Jihad, to fight the Soviet occupation of Afghanistan. While in Afghanistan, he met Osama bin Laden.

After leaving Afghanistan, al-Zawahiri went to Russia to set up a base in Chechnya, but was instead arrested — his release followed a few months later. He is also thought to have orchestrated the killing of more than sixty tourists in Luxor, Egypt. In 1998, al-Zawahiri formally merged his Egyptian Islamic Jihad into al-Qaeda, and issued a joint statement with bin Laden. Following the September 11, 2001, terrorist attacks in the United States, al-Zawahiri appeared on the FBI's Most Wanted Terrorists list. That same year, al-Zawahiri published a book that details al-Qaeda philosophy. In June 2011, following the death of bin Laden, al-Zawahiri took over as the leader of al-Qaeda.

As of 2012, his whereabouts remained unknown, but United States authorities suspect he is in Pakistan.

Zahi Hawass

One of the most visible archaeologists in the world, Zahi Hawass was in charge of Egypt's antiquities for nearly ten years before losing his position following the ouster of Mubarak. He is best known in the United States for having appeared in many specials about Egypt, as well as the series *Chasing Mummies* on the History channel.

Born May 28, 1947, Hawass initially planned to study law, but ended up studying archaeology at Alexandria University. He then earned a degree in Egyptology at the University of Cairo, and later earned his Ph.D. in archaeology from the University of Pennsylvania in 1987. He went on to teach Egyptian archaeology, history, and

Zahi Hawass

culture, primarily at the American University in Cairo and the University of California, Los Angeles (UCLA).

In 2002, Hawass was put in charge of the Supreme Council of Antiquities in Egypt. He began an initiative to have foreign countries return antiquities, such as the Rosetta Stone, to Egypt. In exchange, Hawass made it easier for foreign museums to borrow Egyptian artifacts for exhibit, which generated a lot of revenue for the Egyptian government. In addition to his television appearances, Hawass wrote books and gave lectures about mummies and other Egyptian antiquities.

Despite allegations of corruption and harsh treatment of employees, Hawass is credited with spurring interest in Egyptian archaeology in the United States and elsewhere.

FYI FACT:

In 2005, archaeologists discovered the 63rd tomb in the Valley of the Kings – the first one to be discovered there since Tutankhamun's. The site, designated KV-63, is located about 50 feet (15 meters) from the walls of Tut's tomb. On January 25, 2011, the first day of the Egyptian revolution, another tomb was accidentally discovered along the path to King Tut's tomb. With Egypt's government in turmoil, KV-64 wasn't excavated until 2012, when it was determined to be the tomb of a singer named Nehmes Bastet.

Koshary

Ingredients:

2 cups cooked rice
2 cups cooked penne pasta
2 tablespoons white vinegar
1 teaspoon ground cumin
½ teaspoon garlic powder
1 cup cooked lentils
2 cups diced tomatoes
½ cup water
1½ tablespoons sugar
¾ teaspoon ground cinnamon
½ teaspoon salt
¼ teaspoon crushed red pepper
3 cups yellow squash, cut into ½-inch pieces
2 cups thinly sliced onions
1 tablespoon oil
salt and pepper to taste

Instructions:

Prepare the following recipe with **adult supervision:**

1. Combine rice and pasta in large serving platter. Keep warm.
2. Whisk together vinegar, ½ teaspoon cumin, and garlic powder in a medium bowl. Add cooked lentils and stir to combine. Spoon this lentil mix over rice and pasta.
3. Combine tomatoes, water, sugar, cinnamon, salt, remaining ½ teaspoon of cumin, and red pepper in a saucepan. Cook over medium flame until heated through, about 5 minutes, stirring occasionally. Stir in squash, and continue to cook for another 10 minutes.
4. Cook onions in large skillet with one tablespoon oil over medium-high heat, stirring frequently, until lightly browned, about 10 minutes.
5. Spoon the tomato mixture over the lentil layer. Partially stir tomato mixture into other layers, but don't fully combine all layers. Add cooked onions as a topping.
6. Add salt and pepper to taste.

Your Name in Hieroglyphics

Materials
- Self-hardening clay or sand dough
- Plastic spoon and knife

Instructions
1. Flatten the dough into a slab around one-half-inch thick, with with your hands or a rolling pin.
2. Cut the slab into a rectangle with the plastic knife.
3. Using the chart as a guide, spell out your name in hieroglyphics using the knife and spoon to carve the symbols. You can spell your name top to bottom, left to right, or right to left. Vowel sounds were usually left out in Egyptian hieroglyphics (even though they were spoken), unless the word began with a vowel. You will find there may be several different ways to spell your name in hieroglyphics. You can also choose to use the sound instead of the exact letter (for example, for the "ph" sound in hieroglyphics, use the hieroglyph for "f").

HIEROGLYPH	REPRESENTS	PRONOUNCED	HIEROGLYPH	REPRESENTS	PRONOUNCED
	vulture	ah (father)		reed	i (filled)
	two reeds	y (discovery)		arm & hand	broad a (car)
	quail chick	oo (too) or w (wet)		foot	b (boot)
	mat	p (pedestal)		horned viper	f (feel)
	owl	m (moon)		water	n (noon)
	mouth	r (right)		reed shelter	h (hat)
	twisted flax	h! (ha!)		placenta	kh (like Scotch 'loch')
	animal's belly	ch (like German 'ich')		folded cloth	s (saw)
	door bolt	s (saw)		pool	sh (show)
	slope of hill	k (key)		basket with handle	k (basket)
	jar stand	g (go)		loaf	t (tap)
	tethering rope	tj (church)		hand	d (dog)
	snake	dj (adjust)			

BCE

ca. 7000   The first permanent settlers reside in Egypt.

ca. 3500   Rainfall decreases in the Sahara, turning it from a lush savanna to a desert; people begin to establish settlements along the Nile, including Upper and Lower Egypt.

ca. 3100   King Narmer (or Menes) unites Upper and Lower Egypt into country, founding the first Egyptian dynasty.

ca. 2630   Construction begins on the Step Pyramid at Saqqara, designed by Imhotep.

ca. 2550   The Great Pyramid of Giza is completed.

ca. 2200-2150 Drought devastates the Egyptian economy, leading to the collapse of the Old Kingdom, and the re-division of Egypt into two.

1700s   Hyksos enter the Nile delta and take control of the region.

ca. 1334   Tutankhamun takes over the throne of Egypt at age nine, following the death of his father.

ca. 943   Libyans establish the Twenty-second Dynasty.

700s   The Nubians conquer Egypt, founding the Twenty-fifth Dynasty.

525   Persians invade Egypt.

332   Alexander the Great of Greece conquers Egypt and founds the city of Alexandria.

323   Upon the death of Alexander the Great, Ptolemy is appointed ruler of Egypt, establishing the Ptolemaic dynasty.

196   The Rosetta Stone is carved.

51   Ptolemy XII dies, Cleopatra becomes queen.

31   Octavian defeats Antony and Cleopatra in the Battle of Actium.

30   Egypt becomes a province of the Roman Empire.

CE

642   Arabs conquer Egypt, taking the country from the Romans, and making Egypt a part of the Islamic Empire.

969   Cairo founded as Egypt's capital.

1154-1169	Christian Crusaders invade Egypt.
1174	Saladin becomes the sultan of Egypt forming the Ayyubid dynasty.
1250	The Mamelukes seize control of Egypt.
1516	Ottoman soldiers invade Egypt, making it part of the Ottoman Empire.
1799	Napoleon invades Egypt, taking control of the country for three years.
1805	Mohammed Ali establishes himself as pasha of Egypt.
1859	Construction of the Suez Canal begins.
1882	The British invade Egypt to control the Suez Canal.
1914	Egypt becomes a British protectorate.
1922	Egypt is formally granted independence from Britain; the Egyptian constitutional monarchy is established, ruled by King Fuad.
1945	Egypt forms the Arab League with other Arab nations.
1952	King Farouk is overthrown by army officers led by Gamal Abdel Nasser.
1953	Egypt is declared a republic.
1967	The Six-Day War begins on June 5.
1971	President Anwar Sadat changes official name of country to Arab Republic of Egypt and introduces a new constitution.
1981	Vice President Hosni Mubarak takes over as president following the death of President Sadat.
2005	Egypt's first competitive presidential elections are held; Mubarak is re-elected amidst accusations of voter fraud.
2011	Protesters force President Mubarak's resignation, leading to the establishment of a transitional government.
2012	Courts disband elected Parliament, returning rule to the military; the first elections of post-revolution Egypt are held; on September 11, Egyptian protesters attack the U.S. Embassy in Cairo.

Introduction

1. World Bank, "Rural Electrification Funds," http://ppp.worldbank.org/
   public-private-partnership/sector/energy/laws-regulations/
   rural-electrification-funds

2. Martin Meredith, *The Washington Post,* "The Fate of Africa," January
   20, 2006. http://www.washingtonpost.com/wp-dyn/content/
   discussion/2006/01/11/DI2006011101372.html

Chapter 1: The Jewel of the Nile

1. American Geophysical Union, *ScienceDaily,* "Sahara's Abrupt
   Desertification Started By Changes In Earth's Orbit, Accelerated By
   Atmospheric And Vegetation Feedbacks," July 12, 1999. http://www.
   sciencedaily.com/releases/1999/07/990712080500.htm

Chapter 2: Land of the Pharaohs

1. Alex Stone, *Discover Magazine,* "Swimming in the Sahara," October
   2006. http://discovermagazine.com/2006/oct/sahara-desert-savanna-climate

2. Ibid.

Chapter 5: Walk Like an Egyptian

1. Tour Egypt, "Egyptian Arabic," http://www.touregypt.net/
   featurestories/arabic.htm

2. Carla N. Daughtry, *Michigan Today,* "Greenness in the Field," Fall 1997.
   http://michigantoday.umich.edu/97/Fal97/mt14f97.html

Chapter 6: Culture

1. Cairo Opera House, "The National Cultural Centre," http://www.
   cairoopera.org/about.aspx

Chapter 7: Economy and Commerce

1. Henry J. Reske, *Newsmax,* "Egypt's Poverty, Unemployment, Push
   Youths to Breaking Point," January 31, 2011. http://www.newsmax.
   com/Newsfront/Egypt-poverty-unemployment-unrest/2011/01/31/
   id/384555

Blackaby, Susan. *Cleopatra: Egypt's Last and Greatest Queen.* New York: Sterling, 2009.
Englar, Mary. *Nefertiti of Egypt.* Mankato, MN: Snap Books, 2009.
Hart, George. *Ancient Egypt.* New York: DK Children, 2008.

On the Internet
Ancient Egypt for Kids
    http://egypt.mrdonn.org/
Ancient Egypt Kid Connection
    http://guardians.net/egypt/kids/index.htm
Tour Egypt: "About Egypt"
    http://www.touregypt.net/aboute.htm
U.S. Department of State: "Egypt"
    http://www.state.gov/r/pa/ei/bgn/5309.htm

WORKS CONSULTED

A&E Biography. "Ayman al Zawahiri."
    http://www.biography.com/people/ayman-al-zawahiri-241182
American Geophysical Union. "Sahara's Abrupt Desertification Started By Changes In Earth's Orbit, Accelerated By Atmospheric And Vegetation Feedbacks." *ScienceDaily,* July 12, 1999. http://www.sciencedaily.com/releases/1999/07/990712080500.htm
Cairo Opera House. "The National Cultural Centre." http://www.cairoopera.org/about.aspx
Central Intelligence Agency. "Egypt." *The World Factbook,* 2012.
    https://www.cia.gov/library/publications/the-world-factbook/geos/eg.html
Daughtry, Carla N. "Greenness in the Field." *Michigan Today,* Fall 1997. http://michigantoday.umich.edu/97/Fal97/mt14f97.html
Meredith, Martin. "The Fate of Africa." *The Washington Post,* January 20, 2006.
    http://www.washingtonpost.com/wp-dyn/content/discussion/2006/01/11/DI2006011101372.html
Reske, Henry J. "Egypt's Poverty, Unemployment, Push Youths to Breaking Point." *Newsmax,* January 31, 2011. http://www.newsmax.com/Newsfront/Egypt-poverty-unemployment-unrest/2011/01/31/id/384555
Roebuck, Carl. *The World of Ancient Times.* Charles Schribner's Sons Publishing: New York, 1966.
Stone, Alex. "Swimming in the Sahara." *Discover Magazine,* October 2006. http://discovermagazine.com/2006/oct/sahara-desert-savanna-climate
Tour Egypt. "Egyptian Arabic."
    http://www.touregypt.net/featurestories/arabic.htm
World Bank. "Rural Electrification Funds."
    http://ppp.worldbank.org/public-private-partnership/sector/energy/laws-regulations/rural-electrification-funds
Zahi Hawass (Official Site). "Biography of Zahi Hawass."
    http://www.drhawass.com/biography

PHOTO CREDITS: All photos—cc-by-sa-2.0. Every effort has been made to locate all copyright holders of material used in this book. If any errors or omissions have occurred, corrections will be made in future editions of the book.

Cataract (KAT-uh-rackt): a large waterfall; fast-moving water or rapids

Consort (KON-sort): the husband or wife of the reigning king or queen

Cursive (KUR-siv): handwritten script, with connected letters

Desertification (deh-zer-ti-fi-KAY-shun): the process by which land turns into desert due to a loss of moisture

Oasis (oh-AY-sis): a fertile area in a desert where water is found from either a well or a natural spring

Pasha (PAH-shah): a Turkish military leader or high-ranking official

Pleistocene (PLAY-stuh-seen): the geological time period that began 2.6 million years ago, and ended 11,700 years ago; characterized by periods of global cooling and glacial cover

Savanna (suh-VAN-nuh): a tropical or subtropical grassland with scattered trees and seasonal rainfall

INDEX

Kathleen Tracy has been a journalist and author for more than 20 years. She has traveled extensively throughout her career, traveling throughout Europe, the South Pacific, and Central America. The author also lived in North Africa for two months while researching an article on movie production, spending extensive time in Tunisia and Egypt.

Harris County Public Library
Houston, Texas